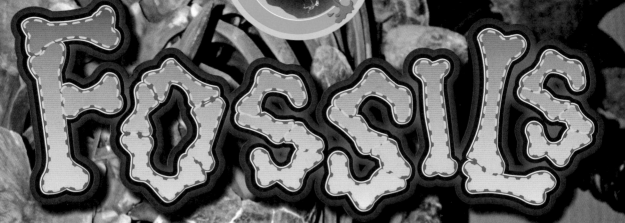

Fossils

Megan Lappi

www.av2books.com

AV² provides enriched content that supplements and complements this book. Weigl's AV² books strive to create inspired learning and engage young minds in a total learning experience.

Your AV² Media Enhanced books come alive with...

Audio
Listen to sections of the book read aloud.

Key Words
Study vocabulary, and complete a matching word activity.

Video
Watch informative video clips.

Quizzes
Test your knowledge.

Embedded Weblinks
Gain additional information for research.

Slide Show
View images and captions, and prepare a presentation.

Try This!
Complete activities and hands-on experiments.

... and much, much more!

Go to **www.av2books.com**, and enter this book's unique code.

BOOK CODE

S 3 2 7 6 5 4

AV² by Weigl brings you media enhanced books that support active learning.

Published by AV² by Weigl
350 5th Avenue, 59th Floor
New York, NY 10118
Website: www.av2books.com

Library of Congress Control Number: 2015938070

ISBN 978-1-4896-4081-9 (hardcover)
ISBN 978-1-4896-4082-6 (softcover)
ISBN 978-1-4896-4083-3 (single user eBook)
ISBN 978-1-4896-4084-0 (multi-user eBook)

Printed in the United States of America in Brainerd, Minnesota
1 2 3 4 5 6 7 8 9 0 19 18 17 16 15

072015
170715

Project Coordinator Heather Kissock
Art Director Terry Paulhus

Photo Credits
Every reasonable effort has been made to trace ownership and to obtain permission to reprint copyright material. The publishers would be pleased to have any errors or omissions brought to their attention so that they may be corrected in subsequent printings.

Weigl acknowledges Getty Images, Alamy, and iStock as its primary image suppliers for this title.

Contents

Studying Fossils

Fossils are the rocklike remains of ancient animals and plants. A fossil can be a hard part of an animal, such as a shell, bone, or tooth. It can also be a footprint that was left behind in mud.

Fossils are usually found in sedimentary rock, a type of rock made of layers of **sediment**. Over millions of years, sedimentary rock builds up, burying fossils. The word "fossil" comes from the Latin word *fossilis*, which means "dug up."

Millions of plant and animal **species** have lived on Earth during the past 3 billion years. Many of these species, such as dinosaurs, are now **extinct**. Scientists study fossils to learn about the creatures and plants that lived in the past. Fossils give scientists information about when and how these plants and animals lived. However, fossils have not been found for many species. Scientists may never find fossils for some types of plants and animals.

Over time, even trees can become fossils.

ANCIENT BONES

Dinosaur fossils have been discovered on **every continent**.

Every seven weeks, a **new kind of dinosaur** is named.

The largest **fossil shark**, called Megalodon, was **45 feet** (14 meters) long.

Fossils of a **giant snake** that lived 58 million years ago have been found in Colombia, South America. It was more than **40 feet** (12 m) long and weighed more than **1 ton** (0.9 metric tons).

Colombia

How Fossils Are Formed

Most animals and plants do not become fossils. Many of them decay, or rot. **Scavengers** eat others. If the plants and animals do not rot and are not eaten, they can become fossils in different ways.

Sometimes, an ancient animal can be trapped in ice and frozen. As the ice melts thousands or millions of years later, the body is revealed. Then, people discover it. Sometimes, an animal dies in a hot and dry place. Its body quickly loses the water that was in it. This loss of water and other changes create a fossil.

A fossil can also form when a plant or the body of a dead animal is covered by mud or sand. Over time, sediment covers the body or plant. The weight of the sediment puts pressure on the hardest parts of the body. They harden into rock. After thousands of years, these parts become fossils.

1

2

FORMING A FOSSIL

One common way that fossils form involves **minerals**. Many of the fossils that scientists have discovered were created in this way.

1 An animal dies in a place that scavengers cannot reach.

2 Sediment covers the body. Sometimes, this happens gradually. Sometimes, floods full of sediment wash over the body. They cover it in a thick layer of dirt, rock, and other material.

3 Over millions of years, more layers of sediment pile up on top of the body. Parts of the body decay, including spaces within the bones. Minerals enter these spaces and harden. They gradually replace parts of the body. These parts become as hard as stone.

4 Earth's surface moves, splitting the sediment layers. The body, now a fossil, is exposed to view.

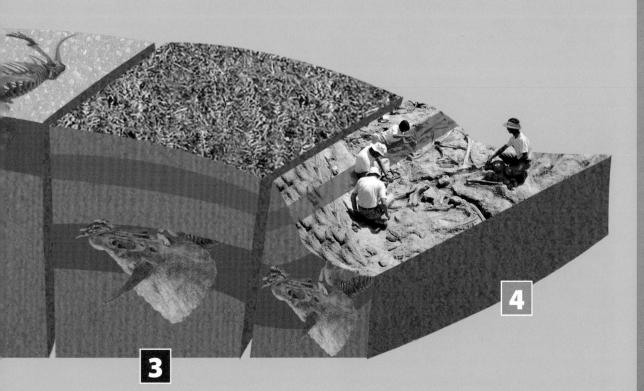

3

4

Fossils over Time

Scientists have divided Earth's history into blocks of time called eras. Different types of animals lived during each era. Scientists can tell which era an animal lived in from the layer of rock that contains its fossils. Fossils found in upper layers are younger than fossils found in lower layers.

ARCHEAN ERA

- Began 4 billion years ago.
- Living things made up of one **cell** appear in Earth's oceans.
- Some **algae** begin to grow. These are called stromatolites and still exist today.

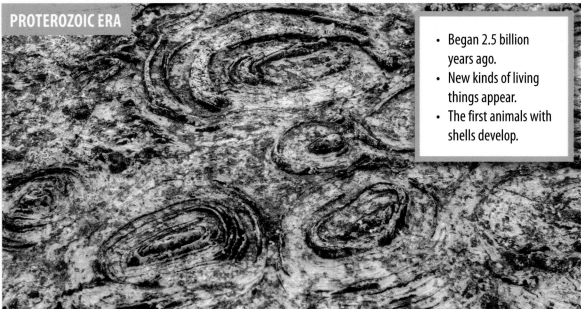

PROTEROZOIC ERA

- Began 2.5 billion years ago.
- New kinds of living things appear.
- The first animals with shells develop.

PALEOZOIC ERA

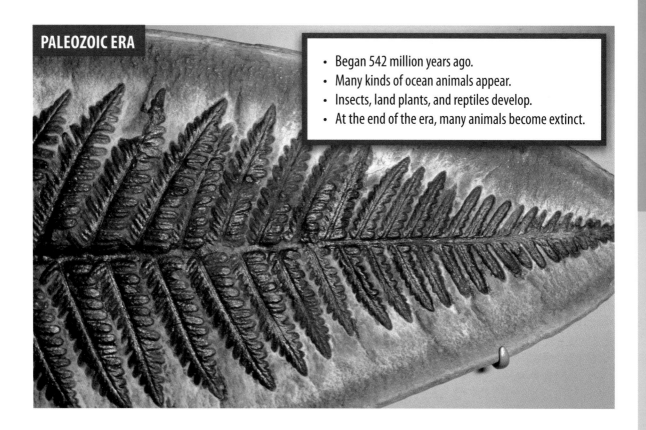

- Began 542 million years ago.
- Many kinds of ocean animals appear.
- Insects, land plants, and reptiles develop.
- At the end of the era, many animals become extinct.

MESOZOIC ERA

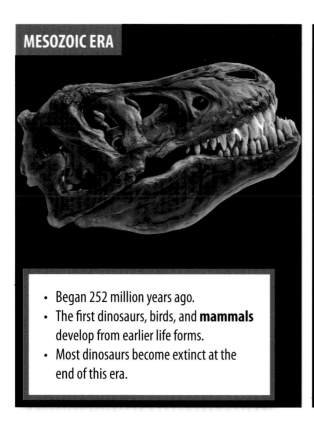

- Began 252 million years ago.
- The first dinosaurs, birds, and **mammals** develop from earlier life forms.
- Most dinosaurs become extinct at the end of this era.

CENOZOIC ERA

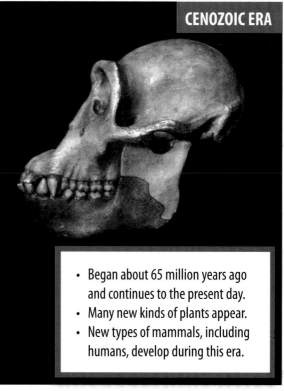

- Began about 65 million years ago and continues to the present day.
- Many new kinds of plants appear.
- New types of mammals, including humans, develop during this era.

The Bone Wars to Find Fossils

The first dinosaur bones were found in the 1820s in England. At first, people did not know what they had discovered. They thought that the bones belonged to an extinct lizard. However, scientists soon realized that these bones were different from those of any other animals.

Creatures that people did not know about must have once lived on Earth. In 1842, British scientist Sir Richard Owen called these creatures Dinosauria. This word means "terrible lizards."

Study of Fossils through History

1000s

1700s

1800s

1823 Human bones are found with bones from a woolly mammoth. This evidence shows that humans and mammoths lived at the same time tens of thousands of years ago.

1027 Avicenna first suggests that liquids carrying minerals might form fossils. He was a scientist living in the area called Iraq today.

1770 Fossil bones of Mosasaurs are found in the Netherlands in Europe. Mosasaurs are giant extinct lizards.

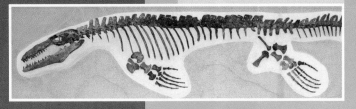

In the 1870s, a number of dinosaur bones were discovered in Wyoming and Colorado. Two men began to compete to find the most fossils and identify the most types of dinosaurs. Their names were Othniel Charles Marsh and Edward Drinker Cope. Their rivalry was called the "Bone Wars." Between them, the two men uncovered more than 130 dinosaur species and thousands of bones. Before and after the Bone Wars, many other scientists also made important fossil discoveries.

In some areas, students can join field trips led by scientists to find and dig up fossils.

1800s

1900s

2000s

1974 Scientist Donald Johanson discovers a fossil that is nearly 3.2 million years old. The fossil, which is closely related to humans, is named "Lucy."

1855 The fossil of a feathered dinosaur-like animal, archaeopteryx, is found in Germany.

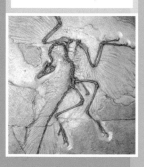

1990 The most complete fossil skeleton ever found of a Tyrannosaurus rex dinosaur, nicknamed Sue, is uncovered in South Dakota.

2009 The fossil of a Dreadnoughtus is completely uncovered. When alive, this dinosaur was 85 feet (26 m) long.

FOSSILS
around the World

ARCTIC
OCEAN

NORTH
AMERICA

ATLANTIC
OCEAN

PACIFIC
OCEAN

SOUTH
AMERICA

Name: Smilodon
Location: Los Angeles, California
Fast Fact: This big cat, nearly twice the size of today's lions, became extinct about 11,000 years ago.

Name: Albertosaurus
Location: Red Deer River, Alberta, Canada
Fast Fact: This large, meat-eating dinosaur lived about 75 million years ago.

Name: Titanosaur
Location: Patagonia, Argentina
Fast Fact: Thousands of eggs were discovered at Auca Mahuevo. Some held complete skeletons of young titanosaurs.

Legend

N

620 Miles

0   1,000 Kilometers

• Major fossil site

FIND OUT MORE ABOUT FOSSILS

This map shows locations around the world where major fossil discoveries have been made. Use this map, and research online to answer these questions.

1. On what continent have the largest numbers of fossils been found?
2. In which country have the most dinosaur fossils been found?

ARCTIC OCEAN

Name: Pliosaur
Location: Weymouth Bay, Great Britain
Fast Fact: This sea reptile could be as much as 85 feet (26 m) long.

Name: Archaeopteryx
Location: Solnhofen, Germany
Fast Fact: Archaeopteryx, which lived about 150 million years ago, is the oldest fossil of a bird ever found.

EUROPE

ASIA

AFRICA

PACIFIC OCEAN

Name: Velociraptor
Location: Gobi Desert, Mongolia
Fast Fact: A large claw on each foot allowed this dinosaur to slash at its prey.

AUSTRALIA

SOUTHERN OCEAN

Name: Fossil footprints
Location: Lake Quarry, Queensland, Australia
Fast Fact: More than 3,000 fossil dinosaur footprints were found in the mud at the bottom of a lake.

ANTARCTICA

Amber, Tar Pits, and Footprints

Sometimes, only the hard parts of a plant or animal turn into a fossil. At other times, a whole plant or animal is **preserved**. Then, scientists can see exactly what the plant or animal looked like when it was alive.

Millions of years ago, sticky sap oozed from pine trees. Sometimes, an insect or plant seed became stuck in the sap. Over time, the sap hardened. It became another type of fossil called amber. Amber is yellow and looks like glass. Pieces of amber with fossils of insects or seeds inside them are studied by scientists. They want to find out how these insects or seeds are different from those of today.

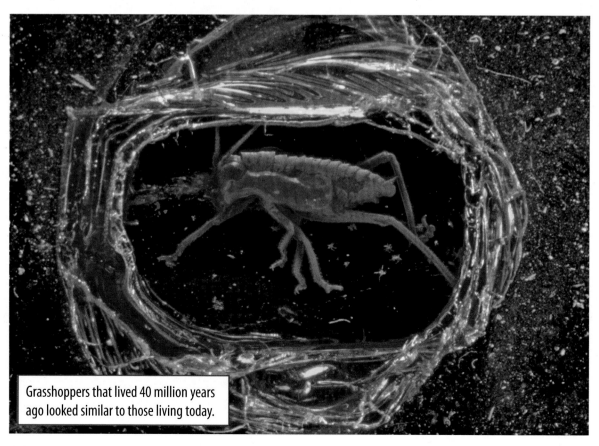

Grasshoppers that lived 40 million years ago looked similar to those living today.

Animals also became trapped in tar pits and died. Tar pits are lakes that contain asphalt, the same sticky material used to make roads. Over time, the animals' skin and flesh decayed. However, their bones and teeth remained. Whole skeletons have been discovered in tar pits.

Trace fossils show an animal's activity. Footprints left in mud are trace fossils. It is more common to find trace fossils than fossils of an entire body. One animal can leave thousands of traces behind. Trace fossils can tell scientists how fast an animal moved. They can also reveal the animal's size. A large animal's footprints are spaced far apart. They are often deep because of the animal's weight. A small animal's footprints are close together and not very deep. If many animal footprints are found together, scientists know that these animals lived in **herds**.

MAKE YOUR OWN FOOTPRINT

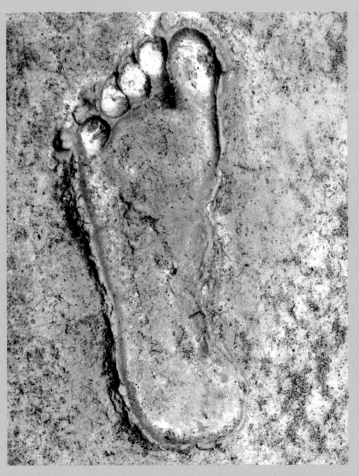

You can make your own fossil footprint. You will need clay, a piece of cardboard, and a rolling pin or large smooth bottle.

Step 1
Place the clay on the cardboard.

Step 2
Using the rolling pin or bottle, smooth and flatten the clay. The clay should be about 2 inches (5 centimeters) thick.

Step 3
Take off one shoe and sock. Press your bare foot into the clay to make a footprint.

Step 4
Now, set the clay aside to harden.

Step 5
After a few days, the clay will be as hard as stone. One day, it will be a fossil.

Taking Care of Fossils

Some scientists spend many years searching for fossils in areas around the world. Once a fossil is discovered, scientists and the team of people working with them remove it from the ground. Digging up a fossil is difficult. Team members must be careful not to damage it. First, they use tools to clear away the rock, sand, or soil around the fossil. Then, photographs are taken and pictures are drawn showing where the fossil was found. Scientists study these images later.

Before fossil bones are moved, they often are wrapped in layers of cloth dipped in plaster. When the plaster hardens, it protects the fossil from damage during shipping. Fossil bones from a large animal are labeled to show the part of the animal's body it came from.

Scientists have found a number of fossils in the Grand Staircase-Escalante National Monument region of southern Utah.

Fossils usually are sent to a museum or university to be studied. There, scientists remove the plaster. Then, they use small tools to carefully remove any rock or soil that may still be on the fossil. Once all the rock is removed, the fossil bones of an animal may be put together to try to show the animal's whole skeleton.

Fossil bones may be very heavy or may break easily. To keep the original fossil pieces safe, workers sometimes make copies of them. The copies can be used for study or put on display. The Tyrannosaurus rex skeleton named Sue went to the Field Museum in Chicago, Illinois. Workers at the museum spent a total of 30,000 hours cleaning and making exact copies of 250 of the dinosaur's bones and teeth.

42 FEET
Length of the skeleton of the Tyrannosaurus rex Sue. (13 m)

67 million
years ago
Time period when Sue lived.

5
FEET
Length of Sue's skull. (1.5 m)

What Did Dinosaurs Look Like?

Scientists have some information about what the skin of certain dinosaurs looked like. They have found fossil imprints of dinosaur skin. These imprints were made in mud or clay that later hardened. Some imprints show features that look like feathers. Other imprints show a pebbly surface or skin with knobs sticking out.

However, scientists have no way of knowing a dinosaur's skin color. Some scientists think that plant-eating dinosaurs may have had uneven patterns on their skin. These patterns would have helped the animals to be **camouflaged** as they ate in forests or grasslands. **Predators**, such as Tyrannosaurus rex, would have found it harder to see the plant eaters. Some scientists think that meat-eating dinosaurs were brightly colored. This coloring would have warned off predators or helped possible mates find each other.

Some dinosaurs had bone-like plates called scutes sticking up from their skin. The scutes provided protection.

What Is a Paleontologist?

The scientists who search for and study fossils are known as paleontologists. They are interested in science. Paleontologists must be patient because they may spend years doing field work before making a major fossil discovery. Future paleontologists study geology, biology, chemistry, physics, and math in college. Many receive a master's or doctorate degree.

Paleontologists may use power saws to cut away extra plaster before a fossil is shipped.

Tools

Geologic maps show the kinds and ages of rock on Earth's surface. They help paleontologists find likely places to search for fossils. Paleontologists use shovels, picks, and jackhammers to remove large chunks of dirt and rock around a fossil. Then, they use tiny dental picks, toothbrushes, and dry paintbrushes to clean off the fossil.

Safety

Paleontologists often search for fossils in remote areas and in harsh climates. They use tablet computers or other devices with global positioning system (GPS) software. Paleontologists need proper clothing for the weather in which they are working.

Fossil Finds

65 tons
Weight of Dreadnoughtus, the largest known land dinosaur. (59 metric tons)

0.007 inches
Size of the tiniest fossil ever found. (0.017 cm)

3.5 billion years
Age of the oldest fossil ever found.

Fossil Quiz

Now that you have read all about fossils, test your knowledge by answering these questions. All of the information can be found in the text you just read. The answers are provided below for easy reference.

1 What type of scientist searches for and studies fossils?

4 Which two scientists competed in the "Bone Wars"?

7 In what kind of rock are fossils usually found?

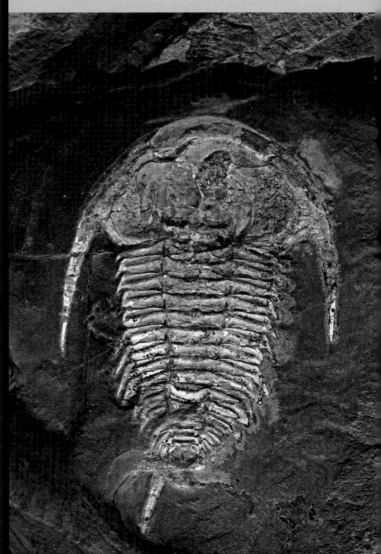

2 In which era of Earth's history did the first dinosaurs appear?

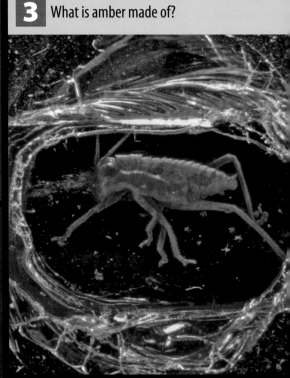

5 What do trace fossils show?

6 When were fossils first discovered?

8 What is the oldest fossil of a bird ever found?

9 What is the size of the smallest fossil ever found?

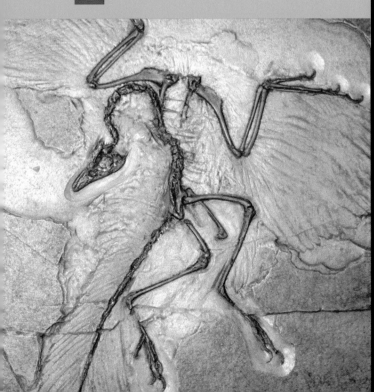

10 What does "fossil" mean in Latin?

Science in Action

F ollow these instructions to create your own fossil. A fossil can be made from something as simple as a leaf found in your neighborhood.

BEFORE YOU START, YOU WILL NEED:

Water

Soil

Small pail

Leaf or shell

Spoon

Baking pan

Making Your Own Fossil

1 Using the spoon, mix the water and soil together in the pail until they form a thick mud. Use more soil than water.

2 Carefully mix a leaf or shell into the mud. Make sure it is hidden in the mud.

3 Pour the mixture into the baking pan.

4 Let the mud dry in sunlight.

5 After the mud has dried, gently break it open.

6 Observe the imprint the object made in the mud. Can you tell what the object is just by looking at its imprint?

Key Words

algae: plantlike life forms made up of one or more cells

camouflaged: hidden or disguised

cell: the smallest unit that all living things are made of

extinct: no longer alive anywhere on Earth

herds: groups of animals that live and travel together

mammals: animals that have hair or fur and that feed mother's milk to their young

minerals: solid materials found in nature that are not plants or animals

predators: animals that hunt other animals for food

preserved: prevented from decaying

scavengers: animals that feed on dead animals

sediment: material from stone or sand carried by water, wind, or moving sheets of ice

species: a group of the same kind of living things, whose members can produce young

Index

Log on to www.av2books.com

AV² by Weigl brings you media enhanced books that support active learning. Go to www.av2books.com, and enter the special code found on page 2 of this book. You will gain access to enriched and enhanced content that supplements and complements this book. Content includes video, audio, weblinks, quizzes, a slide show, and activities.

AV² Online Navigation

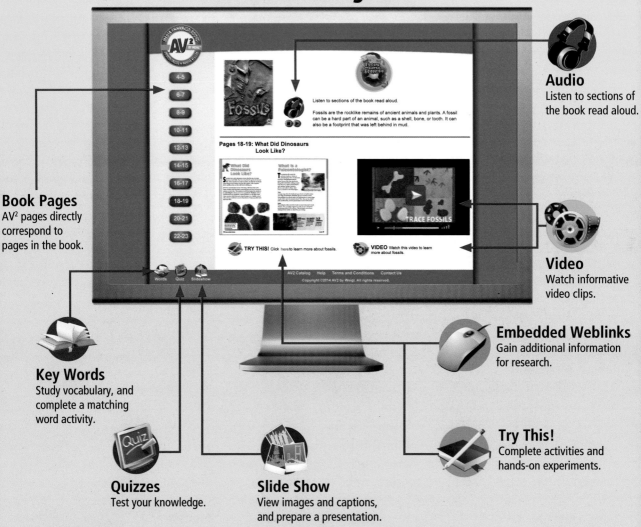

Audio
Listen to sections of the book read aloud.

Book Pages
AV² pages directly correspond to pages in the book.

Video
Watch informative video clips.

Key Words
Study vocabulary, and complete a matching word activity.

Embedded Weblinks
Gain additional information for research.

Try This!
Complete activities and hands-on experiments.

Quizzes
Test your knowledge.

Slide Show
View images and captions, and prepare a presentation.

AV² was built to bridge the gap between print and digital. We encourage you to tell us what you like and what you want to see in the future.

Sign up to be an AV² Ambassador at www.av2books.com/ambassador.

Due to the dynamic nature of the Internet, some of the URLs and activities provided as part of AV² by Weigl may have changed or ceased to exist. AV² by Weigl accepts no responsibility for any such changes. All media enhanced books are regularly monitored to update addresses and sites in a timely manner. Contact AV² by Weigl at 1-866-649-3445 or av2books@weigl.com with any questions, comments, or feedback.